TABLE OF CONTENT

INTRODUCTION

MINDFULNESS EVERYDAY

PART 1

Introduction

AS MINDFULNESS AND MEDITATION PRACTICES have become increasingly mainstream, more and more people are actively seeking resources for how to incorporate these tools into their lives. But many of the existing books on the subject are centered on the whys of practice, including evidence-based bene ts; they don't truly serve the beginner who's diving into practice for the rst time. Many students have practical questions and share common concerns— everything from preventing the mind from wandering, to what to do if you really need to scratch your nose, to what you have to be, do, and have in order to "do it right."

There are a few practical guides out there, but even those are lacking in depth (and frankly, they're not very exciting to read). In this guide, I've drawn on my traditional training and my years of experience working with students to create a practical and straightforward approach to mindfulness, including a variety of options that cater to di erent personalities and lifestyles.

When I rst sat down in a meditation class as an adult, I was struck by the fact that everyone in the room seemed to be completely at ease. At 18 years old, struggling with drug addiction, I had found a group of people who exuded a kind of calm acceptance that I could only dream of. At the time, my moment-to-moment experience was one of stress, chaos, and pain. I did not know exactly what I was searching for, but I knew I wanted to feel the way these people seemed to feel.

When I got sober a year later, I dived head rst into meditation and mindfulness practice. I engaged with a local meditation community and began to see the ways in which I had been causing my own su ering and pain. Like all people, I've had painful experiences in my life. Some were caused by my own behavior; others were out of my control.

My first big insight came when I realized that my reactions to these experiences were causing me more pain than the experience itself.

As the years passed by, my meditation practice became an increasingly important part of my life. I didn't have much money, so I attended a donation-based silent meditation retreat in Southern California when I was 19. For 10 days, I followed instruction and sat in silence. I felt massively underequipped and overwhelmed. I struggled daily with consistent thoughts of leaving early and constantly fought with the discomfort I felt in both mind and body. It was rough.

But when that retreat ended, I immediately signed up for another one scheduled a few months later. Although I never experienced a "white-light" moment, something continued to draw me toward the practice. Since then, I've attended ("sat") multiple retreats a year, ranging from seven days to four weeks.

Discipline has never been a strong suit of mine. It took a lot of e ort to start meditating regularly, but as the months and years accumulated, I began to notice the bene ts of practice showing up in my day-to-day life. Anger, anxiety, and harsh self-talk still came up, of course. But I found myself able to meet these experiences with awareness and patience rather than frustration and pain. Although I still had unpleasant emotional experiences, I didn't feel so strongly swayed by every situation or thought.

In 2014, I got the opportunity to lead some meditation groups at Against the Stream in Santa Monica, California. I lled in for the weekly Sunday group and was a part of an awesome team that taught a group for teenagers. In 2015, two of my teachers nominated me to teach meditation for a program at Spirit Rock Meditation Center, one of the most well-respected meditation centers in the West. This o ered me the opportunity to work with inspiring teachers, cultivate my own practice, and explore what it meant to lead a meditation community.

When I opened the One Mind Dharma meditation center in 2017, I did so with one goal in mind: to create a space where anyone could come and investigate their inner experience in a safe, supportive environment. The community has done most of the work, showing up with vulnerability and honesty, and my role as the leader of the community is a powerful o ering for my own practice.

When I rst started practicing, I didn't fully understand what kept pulling me—I just had a faint notion that the way I'd been living was not working. I'd been ghting with every thought, resisting my emotions, and obsessing over past experiences and what I would do in the future. Without knowing exactly what it was that needed to change, I knew deep inside there must be a healthier way to live.

Like you, I'm human. I don't respond mindfully in every moment of every day. My brain goes on autopilot; I worry; I get frustrated. Today, my practice is to observe these experiences, remembering that I have a choice in how I respond. Before I embraced mindfulness, I was driven by instinctual and habitual reactions. But the more I cultivated awareness, the less enslaved I became to my eeting thoughts and emotions. Instead, I can jump in and hit the Pause button, calm myself, and handle stressful situations with con dence and ease. In a sense, mindfulness practice has given me back my free will.

My deepest intention is to make these practices available to anyone who seeks a di erent, more balanced way of living. I have seen people from all walks of life turn to mindfulness for help with anxiety, grief, and physical pain. Regardless of why someone comes to practice, they generally all have the same goal that I did—to nd a healthier way to be a human being.

When I was new to practice, the books I read, teachers I encountered, and classes I took gave me a blueprint to get started. Without those resources, it would've taken me even longer to incorporate a regular practice. My hope is that you can use this book as your own blueprint. I cannot give you a secret key to some advanced state of mindfulness; your work lies in curiosity, re ection, and, yes, a little bit of e ort.

With a little direction, we all have the potential to live with more ease. May the exercises contained between these covers o er you a path to freedom in your life.

Mindfulness Everyday

WHEN I WAS 14 YEARS OLD, my dad gave me a copy of The Miracle of Mindfulness, a book by the Zen monk Thich Nhat Hanh. At the time, I was struggling with bipolar disorder and addiction, and the book o ered a simple introduction to mindfulness practices, which my dad thought would help. As I read through the pages and practices, I was immediately drawn in by the beauty and simplicity of mindfulness meditation. I read each chapter carefully, seeking to fully understand the idea of mindfulness. Reading introduced me to the path, but I never practiced the tools o ered in the book—I imagined that the principles would just seep into my daily life magically. It was years before I began taking action and seeing the bene ts promised in the book.

I learned, as you will, that living mindfully requires a lot of practice. You don't start with perfect awareness and attention. First, you must understand what you are doing, why you are practicing, and how to actually practice. As you learn about the practices, try to apply them to your everyday life as much as you can.

Mindfulness calls for action. It calls for personal investigation.

People all over the world discover mindfulness as a tool to help with anxiety, anger, grief, and many other di cult experiences humans go through. This ancient practice has evolved over millennia and is now more accessible than ever. Every day, we understand more about what it means to be mindful and how mindfulness impacts the brain. By understanding what mindfulness is, how it may be bene cial in your life, and how to get started, you are laying a foundation for deep awareness and growth.

In the Moment, Every Moment

You have heard the word mindfulness before; it's featured on magazine covers, mentioned in tness classes, and touted by top business leaders across industries as a tool to enhance productivity. But as mindfulness practice has become more mainstream, the meaning of the word has become clouded. People may encourage mindfulness, or "being present," but what exactly does this entail?

Mindfulness is often described as the practice of simply "being in the present moment." But this is only one aspect of the practice. Resting in the present moment is an important piece—it's the rst step in bringing your attention to whatever is happening here and now, whether it's a thought, a di cult emotion, a task at work, or the breath—but it's just the beginning. When you limit your de nition of mindfulness to the practice of just being present, you overlook several other important aspects.

As you move through the exercises in this book, you will see the terms mindfulness practice and meditation used interchangeably at times. The idea of sitting silently in meditation can be scary if you've never done it before. It is helpful to understand that the word meditation refers to anytime you are putting dedicated e ort forth to be mindful. This may be in a sitting practice or while you are washing dishes. Remember that mindfulness is practiced not just on a meditation cushion; you can introduce mindfulness into any daily activity.

Mindfulness may be more completely understood as being present with clarity, wisdom, and kindness. If you bring your awareness to the present moment with judgment and anger, is that really useful? In order to build a healthy, bene cial mindfulness practice, it's necessary to cultivate several di erent behaviors, attitudes, and skills.

As you dive into mindfulness practice, you will likely discover a deep well of personal strengths—and a few places where you have room to grow. I call these places the growing edges. Try not to be discouraged by these edges—we all have them. Acknowledging and exploring them is how you work toward growth. Every one of your growing edges o ers an opportunity for you to decrease stress and discomfort in your life.

NINE ASPECTS OF MINDFULNESS PRACTICE

You are here because you have made the decision to begin investigating mindfulness. It is a powerful step and one that should be recognized and appreciated. Take a minute to pat yourself on the back.

To begin your journey of understanding mindfulness practice, let's look at the di erent abilities you will be cultivating.

- ◆ BEING FULLY PRESENT. This is the most well-known and basic piece of mindfulness meditation, but it takes time to cultivate. You may have to coax the mind back to the present moment repeatedly as you practice. As you continue to train the mind to be present, you'll nd yourself more naturally able to rest in present-time awareness.

- ◆ SEEING CLEARLY. This aspect of mindfulness may also be understood as a recognition of the experience you are having. When pain arises, you are able to identify it as pain. When anxiety is present, you recognize it as anxiety. You are cultivating the wisdom to clearly see what you are experiencing in the present moment.

- LETTING GO OF JUDGMENT. You may notice your mind labeling something (a feeling, a thought, etc.) as good or bad, right or wrong, positive or negative. In mindfulness practice, you can let go of such value judgments. When a judgment does arise, you can remind yourself that you do not need to believe it. Accept what is present in the mind, including any feelings of "liking" or "disliking" what you nd.

- BEING EQUANIMOUS. Equanimity is the quality of remaining balanced, especially when presented with di cult or uncomfortable circumstances. Whether the experience you are having is easy or di cult, the energy and e ort you bring to it can remain unchanged. In this way, you build inner resilience, learning to move through di cult situations with balance and stability

- ALLOWING EVERYTHING TO BELONG. Life contains a variety of experiences, and you may nd yourself inviting some in while pushing others away. The English monk Ajahn Sumedho often tells his students, "Everything belongs." With mindfulness, you do not need to exclude any thought, emotion, or experience. Pay attention to whatever arises and make space for the uncomfortable moments.

- CULTIVATING BEGINNER'S MIND. When you learn something new, approach it with curiosity and eagerness to understand. As you grow in your understanding of the world around you, you can fall into "autopilot," believing that you know exactly how things work and what you're doing. To support a healthy mindfulness practice, work to cultivate beginner's mind, observing experiences and situations as if it's your rst time. Remain open to new possibilities and watch out for the times when your mind begins closing.

- ◆ BEING PATIENT. Most people come to mindfulness and meditation practice with a goal in mind. They want to relieve some anxiety, deal with daily stressors, or learn to work through anger. It's okay to have an intention, but remember to be patient; clinging to a speci c outcome can hinder your progress. Patience requires a little bit of trust in the practice, in your teacher, and in yourself. Keep your intention in mind and remember that growth takes time.

- ◆ MAKING A FRIEND. Mindfulness is not about beating yourself up. Kindness is an essential part of practice— and that starts by being kind to yourself. Without kindness, you can be reactive and unable to see clearly. When practicing, respond to your experience with gentleness. Act as if your mind is your friend, not an enemy.

- ◆ HONORING YOURSELF. You don't need to clear the mind, be perfectly calm, or be a master of kindness to start practicing mindfulness. Start wherever you are, and honor yourself for being here in the rst place. This is a practice—not a race. You're not being graded, and if you struggle, it doesn't mean there's something wrong with you or your mind. Be true to yourself and allow space for growth.

The exercises contained in the following pages o er practical ways to build these qualities. You can return to these nine factors throughout your practice, recognizing where you have room to grow.

When I sat my rst silent meditation retreat, I was struck by one thing that continued to arise in my mind: judgment. I knew from my training that I should seek to understand the judgment, not judge myself for judging. My retreat teacher suggested that I practice some kindness and forgiveness toward my mind. I really struggled with this— forgiving oneself can be a lifelong challenge—but I committed to an intention to do just that. Years later, this gentleness and kindness toward the thinking mind is an essential piece of my mindfulness practice.

You, too, will experience di cult moments in practice (and in life). You may need to try a few di erent approaches before guring out what works best. Do your best to remain open, and remember to forgive yourself for not always having the answer immediately. As you continue to practice, you will deepen your understanding of what it is you need. You will know intuitively when to return to beginner's mind, when to practice gentleness, and when you are getting knocked o balance.

MINDFULNESS-BASED STRESS REDUCTION

In light of the recent research on the benefits of mindfulness, psychologists and clinicians are incorporating mindfulness into their practices at an increasing rate. In the late 1970s, professor Jon Kabat-Zinn of the University of Massachusetts Medical Center founded the Mindfulness-Based Stress Reduction program. MBSR is a form of mindfulness-based meditations and practices combined with contemporary science. It offers methods for reducing stress, helping treat depression and anxiety, and working with physical pain. In the past 30 years, MBSR has grown into a worldwide program with thousands of teachers and programs available. In the 1990s, an elaboration of Cognitive Behavioral Therapy (CBT), Mindfulness-Based Cognitive Therapy (MBCT), was created to help prevent relapse in people experiencing depression. Therapists mix CBT methodology with mindfulness-based practices to bring awareness to judgment, self-criticism, and rumination.

Psychologists and psychotherapists have found success with mindfulness-based practices for a variety of individuals. Mindfulness-based relapse prevention is being used to help treat addiction. Mindfulness interventions have proven effective in working with post-traumatic stress disorder. And meditation awareness training can increase overall psychological well-being. As the body of research grows, so does our collective understanding of the practice and all its potential benefits. We are just beginning to scratch the surface of how mindfulness can help in clinical settings.

Research-Based Benefits

I recall participating in a meditation group in my teens, hearing a group of people share about the bene ts of mindfulness in their lives. People told stories of mindfulness helping with panic attacks, curbing their anger, and encouraging a more compassionate lifestyle. When talking with them afterward, I found the joy and clarity in their eyes undeniable.

This was a turning point in my life and practice. I saw that mindfulness was a source of contentment and ease in the lives of other human beings. Today, we're lucky to have a body of clinical research to support that.

Mindfulness has been taught for over 2,000 years. People across the world have utilized its practices, discovering the personal bene ts mindfulness can bring. We live in an exciting time—as scienti c understanding has grown in the past century, many of the world's top minds are using modern methods to prove the myriad bene ts of mindfulness meditation.

MINDFUL BENEFITS

Mindfulness has been studied in clinical settings, using brain imaging technology or extensive psychological testing. Although the eld of mindfulness research is relatively new, research teams continue to nd physical evidence of the anecdotal claims meditators have made for centuries. Many studies nd changes in behavior and brain activity after just a few weeks of practice, with participants maintaining the positive e ects up to a year after undergoing a mindfulness-based training program

Understanding the research can ground you in why you're doing this practice in the rst place and give you a glimpse at some of the bene ts you might experience for yourself.

* STRESS REDUCTION. In 2010, a team of researchers analyzed ndings from the past decade and determined that mindfulness was e ective in relieving anxiety and stress. This was true for study participants whether or not they had previously diagnosed anxiety or stress disorders.

* IMPROVED WORKING MEMORY AND FOCUS. Research at the University of California, Santa Barbara, has found that mindfulness helps people stay focused and more e ectively utilize recently learned information. One encouraging nding of the study is that participants reported signi cantly less mind wandering after just two weeks of mindfulness practice.

* PHYSICAL BENEFITS. The physical bene ts of mindfulness are well documented. Research in the past decade has found that regular meditation can help improve digestion, strengthen the immune system,

lower blood pressure, help the body heal faster, and ease in ammation. Mindfulness is not just about taking care of your mind!

- ◆ BETTER SLEEP. According to Harvard Health, research shows that mindfulness can help with falling asleep and staying asleep. Regardless of what time of day you do it, a meditation practice is likely to help with this.

- ◆ CREATIVE PROBLEM SOLVING. In a 1982 study, researchers discovered that meditation can help people solve problems with more creativity. Cultivating stillness in the mind helps you gain the ability to think in new ways, look at problems from a di erent perspective, and work more e ectively toward a solution. As a by-product, this can also help you deal with stress in the family, at work, and in everyday life.

- ◆ FEWER FEELINGS OF LONELINESS. Loneliness is actually correlated to poor health outcomes. In a study at the University of California, Los Angeles, participants experienced less loneliness after just eight weeks of mindfulness practice. This held true whether the individuals were actually alone or surrounded by a group of friends. In addition, those who practiced mindfulness alone still experienced more feelings of connection and contentment. And in January 2018, after a lengthy investigation of loneliness in the United Kingdom, British prime minister Theresa May even appointed a Minister for Loneliness.

- ◆ IMPROVED SELF-ESTEEM. So many of us struggle with this. Mindfulness practice has repeatedly been shown to boost self-esteem across cultural boundaries. It can help you improve your body image, sense of self-worth, and basic contentment with who you are as a person.

- ◆ MOOD REGULATION. Although mindfulness is not a substitute for proper clinical care, it does o er a powerful way to help regulate mood disorders and issues. If you're experiencing periods of depression, anxiety, or mood changes, mindfulness may help you with these issues. Researchers have seen mindfulness help stabilize moods in those with diagnosed mood disorders and those without.

The Essentials of Practice

You don't need anything special or "extra" to cultivate mindfulness in your life. Getting started is usually the most di cult part, but over time, it becomes easier as you nd what works best for you and your lifestyle. As you practice, pay attention to what feels easy, smooth, and "right," and what causes friction and resistance.

Use the practices in this book, the suggestions for getting started, and your own insight to help build a mindfulness practice. Throughout my years of teaching, I have heard of many ways to get started, and they're all slightly di erent—personalized to the individual.

Here are a few things you can do to help yourself get on the road to mindfulness.

ESTABLISHING A PRACTICE

When I was new to meditation, I really struggled to practice; it felt like a chore. But as I practiced more regularly, it became a habit. I even started to look forward to my periods of mindfulness throughout the day. As the bene ts of my practice started showing up in daily life, my con dence and interest in mindfulness grew, and practice became even easier and more enjoyable

All mindfulness requires from you is to show up and put forth a little effort. Below are the essential elements you'll work on as you build your mindfulness practice.

- ◆ MAKING TIME TO MEDITATE. With your busy schedule, it may seem impossible to find the time to meditate. In my experience working with individuals from around the world, this is a common challenge—and yet you can absolutely find time to practice. The key is making mindfulness a priority. A few things that help are setting aside specific time to practice, waking up a few minutes earlier than usual, or setting a calendar reminder to practice in the afternoon. You don't have to dive right into 30 minutes a day; start with 5 minutes.

- ◆ CREATING SPACE TO PRACTICE. You may struggle to find the right place to practice. Remember that this can be done literally anywhere. Let go of the idea that there are "perfect" places or "bad" places. You can also create a dedicated space for meditating—find an area of your home that is relatively quiet and relaxing. If your office or work space is too chaotic, try practicing in your car before going inside. You may also utilize public spaces, like beaches, parks, and quiet roads (if you're comfortable doing so).

- ◆ SETTING AN INTENTION. You wouldn't be here if you didn't have some intention in mind. Why are you interested in finding a more mindful way to live? Whatever your answer, it helps to consistently remind yourself of this deeper intention, connecting with what drives you. The mind may try to convince you not to follow through, or that you don't have time to meditate. Fighting with these thoughts often proves futile. Instead, bring the mind back to your deeper intention. Remember what matters to you.

◆ BUILDING CONSISTENCY. The practices in this book present opportunities to investigate mindfulness in many di erent ways in your life. Try to use at least one every day, always keeping your intention of mindfulness present. Practicing consistently helps you train the mind e ectively. When you practice every day, you build the habit fairly quickly. It's like going to the gym—if you go once a month, you probably won't notice results very quickly. But if you go twice a week, all those short little periods of exercise build on each other, and you grow stronger. Mindfulness is a cumulative practice; the mental muscle gets tter as you continue training.

◆ FINDING A FRIEND. Social support can go a long way toward encouraging new habits. Try asking a friend or family member to practice with you once a day. This will give you a sense of accountability to someone other than yourself, and some external motivation always helps. You'll also have the opportunity to talk about your experience with someone else, which will help you both as you move through practice together.

◆ KEEPING A JOURNAL. Get a journal to use speci cally for your mindfulness practice. After you practice for the day, take a few simple notes. How was your practice? Did anything new or interesting come up? How do you feel? The act of writing down your experience with mindfulness can help you understand it more clearly, ingrain your newfound insight into the mind, and give you something to look back on. I still look back at my rst meditation journal from time to time, and I love seeing the progress I've made over the years.

"Mindfulness is simply being aware of what is happening right now without wishing it were different; enjoying the pleasant without holding on when it changes (which it will); being with the unpleasant without fearing it will always be this way (which it won't)."

Getting the Most out of This Book

This book will serve as a guide for your practice, o ering direction as you get started with mindfulness. I personally use every practice described in this book and have seen them bene t my many students. You may nd that some exercises or ideas are more useful to you than others. Remain open, trying each practice to see how it lands.

The exercises are o ered in three parts: Basic Mindfulness Exercises, Everyday Mindfulness, and Mindful Moods. In each part, the exercises start short and simple. As you progress, the practices will build on previous exercises and require slightly more time. I recommend starting each section from the beginning and taking your time to master the simpler practices before moving on to the next.

If you are a beginner, I recommend starting with Basic Mindfulness Exercises rst, no matter what your speci c concerns are. This part details the foundational practices of mindfulness, and you'll continue to come back to them throughout your practice.

A word on meditation: Most people hear the word meditation and imagine a pious yogi sitting still for hours on end, with a completely empty mind. While seated meditation is certainly an important part of mindfulness practice, it's important to note that every mindfulness exercise in this book is a form of meditation, and there are plenty that don't require you to stop everything and sit quietly with your eyes closed. There are several more-engaged practices, various tools to use during your daily life, and many open-eye exercises. By incorporating both formal meditation and active mindfulness exercises throughout your day, you can lay the groundwork for a rich mindfulness practice.

ADDRESS YOUR ISSUE

Mindfulness and meditation are bene cial tools for almost anyone, and no matter what your speci c issue, incorporating these practices into your life will have a positive e ect on your overall well-being. That said, it is possible to focus your e orts on a speci c issue, and that's how I've divided up the parts of this book.

If you have a speci c di culty you're facing, feel free to jump to those speci c practices and sections. You can follow the exercises in the order I've presented, or skip around to those that call out to you or work best for your lifestyle and schedule.

HOW DO I KNOW IT'S WORKING?

Your first few times meditating may not feel very relaxing. It's incredibly hard to sit still and observe the mind, especially when you first start out. Like any other new habit, it will take time to see results. It's called a practice because it's not meant to have an ending—like crossing a finish line or cooking all the recipes in your favorite cookbook. Mindfulness is not meant to be a quick fix; it will keep you company throughout the rest of your life. As you progress, notice the moments of mindfulness that begin to pop up during your days. You can also tune in to any cravings for results (or a "cure"), and try to view these with curiosity instead of impatience. The

GROW YOUR PRACTICE

The practices contained in this book range in length from just 5 minutes to 20 minutes or longer. As you start the journey, give yourself permission to grow into the longer exercises. As you master the quicker, simpler techniques, your understanding and insight will build, and you can move on to some of the longer ones. This is a path of growth. Be patient with yourself, and move through the exercises at your own speed. I encourage you to try all of the exercises so you can experience all the di erent ways you can cultivate mindfulness.

EXTEND YOURSELF

Moving through the book, you will face challenges and di culties. Some exercises will come naturally, while others may expose growing edges and require more time and e ort. Remember, you are capable. You may doubt yourself in certain moments, but sometimes growth pushes you out of your comfort zone. These practices may lovingly nudge you to dig deeper. It is okay to experience fear, doubt, or judgment. Just keep moving forward with your practice

PRACTICE REGULARLY

Whether or not you have an existing meditation practice, a few minutes of mindfulness during the day is bene cial. Incorporate a practice every day. That consistency will encourage the building of a habit and help deepen your practice. If you have a busy day, nd a short exercise in the book—and remember, the long ones aren't better than the short ones; any practice is a good practice.

The ﬁve-minute exercises will be especially useful as your practice grows. They help refocus you when you start to drift, and they can be a great way to reconnect with your original intention.

FORGIVE FRUSTRATION

Anytime you are learning something new, it's natural to become frustrated. You aren't learning as quickly as you would like, you take three steps forward and two steps back, or you completely forget to practice one day. Not being "good" at something is frustrating—which is why forgiveness and beginner's mind are such important parts of the journey. The path to mindfulness is not a straight, one-way road. It winds, there are stop signs, and you may ﬁnd yourself taking a turn you did not expect. Return to forgiveness and curiosity as many times as it takes

The exercises that follow will help you investigate your own experience. Clarity will grow. You will learn to respond with gentleness. But you will not be pulling anything in from outside of yourself. The exercises work by cultivating that which you already have. Within your own mind and heart are the seeds of kindness, patience, wisdom, and awareness. Water the seeds and watch them blossom.

Definitions

You'll see the following terms peppered throughout the exercises.
FEELING TONE: The experience of something as pleasant, unpleasant, or neutral. For example, the feeling tone of hearing a bird chirp may be pleasant, while the feeling tone of an itch may be unpleasant.
GROWING EDGES: The places where we have room

to grow. These are often difficult moments where we struggle, yet we have a powerful opportunity to learn.

HOOKED IN AND UNHOOKING: Hooking in is when we become enveloped in an experience and lose the power to choose how we respond. Unhooking is the act of releasing from the experience and returning to awareness.

LOVING-KINDNESS: The practice and quality of caring for the well-being of others. Loving-kindness is an opening of the heart, meeting others with kindness. Sometimes also referred to as metta.

MANTRA/PHRASE: Phrases and mantras are used in some practices as an object of awareness. A phrase or mantra is a simple sentence used to cultivate an intention, and it serves as a way to stay focused on a goal.

MEDITATION: Meditation is simply the act of dedicating time to develop a quality of mind or heart, often in silence. Though often done in a sitting practice, meditation may also be done while walking, doing dishes, or eating.

MONKEY MIND: The mental state in which the mind bounces around quickly, much as a monkey does from branch to branch.

NOTING: The practice of mentally saying what we are experiencing. Noting involves silently saying something in our head; it helps us see something clearly without getting hooked in.

PARASYMPATHETIC NERVOUS SYSTEM: The part of the central nervous system responsible for downregulation, including slowing the heart rate, relaxing muscles, and increasing gland activity.

PRESENT-TIME EXPERIENCE: Whatever is happening for us in the present moment. The present-time experience is what is arising into our experience on a moment-to-moment basis. It is always changing, full of different stimuli, and consistently present.

SENSE-DOORS: The six primary senses that can be accessed in our mindfulness practice: smell, taste, hearing, touch/feeling, sight, and thought. The sense-doors are where we experience phenomena arising and passing.

1
Finding the Breath

The body is always breathing, and the breath is constantly moving. Your breath is not only the best place to start; it's a constant you can return to anytime you need a little centering.

The body is always breathing, and the breath is constantly moving. Your breath is not only the best place to start; it's a constant you can return to anytime you need a little centering.

Find a comfortable position for the body. Sitting is often recommended, as it helps keep the body awake and energized. You can also try lying at on your back, or standing. You may sit on a yoga mat, meditation cushion, or chair. Find what feels comfortable and sustainable for a few minutes of stillness.

Gently allow the eyes to close. If you're more comfortable with the eyes open, try softly gazing at the oor or ceiling (depending on your position). Allow the eyes to relax and rest on one spot. The idea is to minimize distractions in your practice.

Bring your awareness to the abdomen. Relaxing the muscles there, see if you can feel the natural rising and falling. Imagine the body is breathing itself. From the navel around to the obliques, notice the movement with each breath. Take a few deep breaths like this.

Move your awareness up to the chest. As you inhale, tune in to the expansion of the lungs and the rising of the chest. As you exhale, feel the contraction and movement. See if you can follow the feeling of the breath from the beginning of your inhalation through the end of your exhalation.

Now bring your attention to the nostrils. The feeling of the breath may be more subtle here. Try taking a deep breath to see what is present for you. You may notice a slight tickle at the tip of the nose as you breathe in. You may notice the breath is slightly warmer on the way out.

Rest your awareness on the body breathing in one of these three spots. When the mind wanders, refocus on the direct experience of the breath. Continue to observe the breath for a minute or two.

Wrapping up this period of practice, bring this awareness with you into your daily life. Stay in touch with the breath in your body to help the mind remain present.

THE WANDERING MIND

The natural tendency of the mind is to wander. Even the most accomplished meditators have wandering minds! The brain was designed to process information; it's just doing its job. Rather than seeing this as a problem, approach it as an opportunity to strengthen your mindfulness. Try to bring forgiveness, curiosity, and patience to these moments, and whenever your mind wanders, bring it back to the breath.

2
Points of Contact

The body is always in contact with something, whether it is a chair, the ground, your bed, or the air around you. This offers a powerful way to tune in to your present-time experience. You can be mindful of these points of contact anytime—in meditation or throughout your daily life. The sensations are generally easy to feel, making this an ideal practice for beginners to mindfulness.

> *"Mindfulness is the aware, balanced acceptance of the present experience. It isn't more complicated than that. It is opening to or receiving the present moment, pleasant or unpleasant, just as it is, without either clinging to it or rejecting it."*

You can do this practice in any position, but I recommend trying it while sitting. Close the eyes and bring your awareness to the posture of the body. Make any minor adjustments to help the body be at ease.

Begin by noticing the places where the body is touching something else. Can you feel the contact between your feet and the oor? Pay attention to the physical feeling of the feet. There is nothing special to do. Just observe how the feet feel in this moment.

Continue up to where you can feel the contact between your rear end and the chair or cushion. Notice the contact and pressure of the upper thighs with the chair. Rest your awareness here, mindfully observing what this feels like in the body.

Bring the attention to the hands, however they may be resting. Feel the places where the hands are touching each other, sitting in the lap, or resting on the knees.

Focus on whatever part of the hand is in contact with something else.

Now see where you can feel the sensation of the clothes on the body. You can scan the body to see where this sensation is present. It may be easiest to feel the places where the clothing stops and the skin is exposed, such as the arms, neck, or ankles

Finally, bring your awareness to the sensation of the air on your skin. You may notice the temperature of the air feels di erent on the palm of the hand than on the back of the hand. You may also feel the wind if you are sitting outside. There is no right or wrong. Be true to your own experience.

Finishing this practice, bring mindfulness to the points of contact during the day. Whenever you sit down, feel the body come into contact with the chair. When you stand up, notice your feet on the poor.

DEALING WITH FEELING OVERWHELMED

When you first begin investigating mindfulness of the body, you may notice several sensations grabbing your attention at once. To help keep your mind focused, try using a mental note or simple mantra while observing a specific place in the body. For example, while tuning in to the feet, think, "Feet. Feet. Feet." Or, if you think a command would work better (it sometimes does), try, "Feel my feet. Feel my feet. Feel my feet." Link the rhythm of the words with your inhales and exhales. Congratulations! You're using mantras— it's that simple.

3
The Power of the Mind

The mind is a powerful tool. In mindfulness practice, you learn to train and work with this tool in an intentional, focused way. This practice lets you play with the power of your mind, showing you how to gently coax it in different ways. You'll also witness the mind's auditory and visual thinking patterns

Bring some playfulness and curiosity to this practice, and try not to take yourself too seriously.

For this practice, you will need to close the eyes. Take a moment to notice how the body is resting. Keep the spine as straight as possible and allow the muscles to relax.

With eyes closed, try to bring to mind the room or space in which you are sitting. Can you picture where in the room your body is resting? Try to visualize the room in your mind. Picture the oor, the walls, and any doors. See what else you can bring up to piece together the space in your mind

Letting go of the room, picture yourself somewhere peaceful. It may be a beach, a forest, or wherever your "happy place" is. In the same way, picture the space around you. Try to bring up as many details as possible

Letting go of the visualization, bring to mind a song or tune you know well. Try to hear the words or melody in your head.

Now use the mind to change the experience of hearing the song. Try to turn the volume down, making the song quiet in your head. Turn the volume up a bit. Investigate what it is like to slow the song down or speed it up.

LOSING FOCUS

While meditating, you may notice your concentration slowly leaking. Sometimes you'll lose yourself in a long train of thought for several minutes before you realize you've done so. When you lose focus during any period of meditation, bring your attention back to the last thing you remember observing mindfully, and if that doesn't work, return to the breath. Noticing the mind has wandered off, you have the opportunity to train it to be present. Come back to your practice as many times as necessary

4
Who Is Listening?

In mindfulness practice, the focus is often on the feelings in the body and the thoughts in the mind. However, tuning in to your other senses can facilitate a strong feeling of presence and awareness. Just as you observed the breath in the first exercise, you can use the sounds around you as the object of your awareness.

Sounds come and go throughout your day and offer a consistent focal point for your mindful attention—no matter where you live or what you do for a living, it's nearly impossible to remove all sound. During meditation, investigate the experience of hearing. You can also bring this practice into your life, pausing to listen closely to the sounds around you at any point during your day

Begin by nding a comfortable posture and allowing the eyes to close. Bring your awareness to the breath, but instead of focusing on the physical feeling of breathing, listen to the sound of the body breathing. Inhaling and exhaling through the nostrils, listen closely to any noises coming from the breath.

Open up your awareness to the other sounds present. You may notice sounds of cars passing, noises within your home, or sounds from nature. Whatever is present, tune in to it.

The mind habitually recognizes what it hears. When a car goes by, you immediately know it is a car. Instead of identifying and de ning what each sound is, try to focus on the actual experience of hearing. Imagine your ears as microphones, just picking up sound. Recognize the rising and passing of the noise, how far away it appears, and from what direction it is coming.

As one sound grabs your awareness, tune in to it for a few moments. Experience the sound fully. Then, open the mind and listen for other noises. Hearing mindfully, continue listening, investigating, and opening up

At the end of the period, return to the breath for a minute. Without forcing or straining, encourage the mind to collect itself fully onto the sound of the breath in the body.

Opening the eyes and moving back into your life, maintain some awareness of the sounds in your life. Notice the act of hearing during your day, and let it draw you back into present-time awareness.

DISTRACTING SOUNDS

During periods of practice or in daily life, you may find certain sounds to be distracting. Noises, like construction, birdsong, or people talking loudly, can draw you out of practice. When you find yourself distracted, make the act of hearing part of your practice. Try to remove yourself from judgment or criticism about where the sound is coming from, and imagine you're hearing it for the first time. See if you can remove language from the sound and refrain from immediately identifying the source of the noise. Notice any aversion that arises, but don't resist sounds you cannot control

5
Eating Mindfully

Now we're going to shift away from mindfulness of the body and mindfulness of hearing and jump into the senses of taste, smell, and sight—starting with the food we eat. The celebrated Vietnamese monk Thich Nhat Hanh offers these words: "Let us establish ourselves in the present moment, eating in such a way that solidity, joy, and peace be possible during the time of eating." Eating is an opportunity to nourish your body while nourishing your mindfulness practice.

> *"This is the real secret of life—to be completely engaged with what you are doing in the here and now. And instead of calling it work, realize it is play."*

You can do this practice in any position, but it is helpful to stay still while eating. This minimizes unnecessary stimulus and helps you focus on the experience. You can do this with any food. I recommend starting with something simple, like raisins, berries, or a few of your favorite vegetables

Begin by taking in the food visually. Notice the colors, shapes, and sizes. As you look at the food, notice the urge to start eating. There is nothing wrong with hunger, but allow the cravings to come and go. Return to the sight of the food.

Next, investigate the smell of the food. Some foods may have stronger aromas than others, and you may have to hold the food up to your nose. Be present for the experience of smelling. When the mind begins craving, just return to the smell in front of you.

Before eating, take a brief moment to appreciate the

energy that went into its production. People worked to grow this food and bring it to you. Nature provided nutrients, rainwater, and sunshine. Maybe somebody cooked, cleaned, or packaged it for you. Bring into your mind all of the energy from various sources that came together to create this meal.

Now, slowly pick up the food. If you are using any utensils, tune in to the experience of touch as you feel the utensil. Mindfully feel how the food or utensil feels in your hand. Is the food sti , soft, cold, or warm?

As you put the food in your mouth, notice the desire to chew and swallow quickly. Instead, start by feeling the temperature of the food. Holding the food in your mouth, can you feel the shape?

As you begin chewing, notice the texture of the food. Does it change as you continue to chew? Notice the avors. You may have a hard time doing more than simply labeling what you're eating, such as "It's a raspberry." Try to dig a little deeper. Are there multiple avors present? Pay attention to the changing of avors as you continue to chew.

When you swallow your bite, tune in to the experience of swallowing. What does it feel like as the food moves down the throat? You may also notice the desire to quickly have another bite. Pause and notice if any avor remains in the mouth for a moment.

You can continue eating like this, reminding yourself to slow down and be present. Continue to check in with the sights, smells, tastes, feelings, and thoughts that arise

When you nish eating, allow yourself to feel gratitude for the food that is nourishing your body. Let the mind relax into a state of appreciation for the energy and life.

GROWING IMPATIENT

Mindful eating is an exercise in patience and requires some self-control. As you try to eat slowly, you may come up against a strong desire to begin eating more quickly. Normally, most of us start preparing our next bite of food while still chewing the previous bite. The foundation of mindful eating is to eat slowly. If craving takes over, just pause, breathe, and slow it down.

6
Scanning the Body

Body scans are a foundational mindfulness practice used in many traditions. This practice was first introduced to me by a therapist, but it may also be found in Buddhist traditions, MBSR practices, and yoga classes. By scanning the body, we get to know the feelings we experience more clearly. The mind also learns to rest in the present-time experience and focus on what is in front of us.

Sit in an upright and energized position if you're able to do so. Allow the eyes to close and make any minor adjustments to be comfortable. Take a few deep breaths, arriving in the present-time experience of breathing.

Bring your awareness up to the crown of the head. What can you physically feel up here at the top of the head? You don't need to x anything, gure anything out, or make anything special happen

Continue down to the forehead and brow. You may be able to feel the temperature of the air on the skin, some tension, or maybe the simple, neutral feeling of the skin. Whatever you can feel, tend to it with mindfulness.

Move your awareness to the cheeks and jaw. Moving through the body like this, just rest your awareness, gently observing what you can physically feel

Tune in to the feeling at the nostrils and upper lip. Although you may feel many things here, the breath is generally the most obvious. Feel the sensations of breathing with each inhalation and exhalation.

Next, move into the mouth, focusing on the tongue, lips, and teeth. Notice how the tongue is resting, the sensation of saliva, and any movement in the mouth

Continue to move through the upper body like this. Move the awareness slowly through the neck, out the shoulders, and down to the hands. Rest with each part of the body for a few moments, patiently observing what is present.

Bring the awareness back up to the shoulder blades, and move down the back. Feel the posture of the spine, the muscles in the back, and any expansion and contraction as the body breathes.

Tune in to the front of the torso, starting at the chest. You may feel the clothes on the body or the breath in the body. As you continue down into the abdomen and stomach, you may notice feelings related to hunger or digestion.

Move through the pelvis and hips, down the legs, and into the feet. Notice the points of contact, the feeling in the joints, and any tension that arises.

When you reach the tips of the toes, open up to feel the body as a whole. From head to toe, sit with the experience of having a body. Try to feel the outline of the body, the posture, and the subtle changes as you breathe.

THE BEDTIME BODY SCAN: Body scanning is one of the most useful practices to help encourage sleep. As a bedtime practice, you can do a body scan while lying down. Start at the feet, and slowly move up through the body. Feel the contact of the body with the bed, and focus on bringing gentleness to the body. Breathe into any points of tension, and allow yourself to naturally relax. Don't strain to fall asleep or relax. Try to move from toe to head with a kind awareness.

7
Every Breath Counts

Bodhipaksa, a Tibetan Buddhist author and professor, said this about concentration: "Concentration allows us to really enjoy what we're doing: whether it's being in the country or reading a book, writing, or talking or thinking. Concentration allows us to think more clearly and deeply."

When you first start practicing, you may find the mind wandering quite a bit. Concentration practice helps you train the mind to focus by giving it something to do. Like mindfulness, this takes time. When the mind wanders, you bring it back. Over time, the mind will learn to focus and let go of distracting thoughts on its own

Find a comfortable sitting posture on a chair or cushion. Straighten the spine, but allow the muscles to relax. Brie y check in with the body. Allow the shoulders to drop, soften the muscles of the abdomen, and invite in relaxation

Notice where you can feel the breath in the body. It may be the abdomen, the chest, or the nostrils. For now, pick one place where you can feel the breath most easily. Rest with the sensations of the breath in this one spot

Begin counting the breaths. Inhale and exhale with awareness, and count one. Inhale, exhale, and count two. Continue like this up to eight, then start back at one.

Remember that the counting serves as an aid to practice, giving the mind something extra on which to focus. It is not a competition or measurement of how well you are doing.

When the mind wanders, just come back to the breath. Begin back at one as many times as necessary. Watch out for judgment and let go of any harsh self-talk.

Continue like this, counting the breaths and building focus. When the mind wanders, notice it. When the mind is concentrated, notice this as well!

When 10 minutes have passed, allow the eyes to open. Continue with your day, noticing when your mind is focused or wandering.

SWITCHING THE COUNT

There are many ways to practice with counting the breath. Concentration is an important practice, helping establish mindfulness, focus during meditation, and greater presence in daily life. By making slight adjustments, you can keep this practice interesting and prevent the mind from going into autopilot. Try counting up to eight, then back down to one. Or try counting with each inhale and each exhale—inhale and count one, exhale and count two. You may also change the number to which you count. Investigate for yourself what is useful.

8
The Mindful Body

During mindfulness practice—especially when you're just starting out—the body can grow anxious, restless, or agitated. To help with this, you can learn to respond to those sensations with compassion and gentleness. In this practice, you will work to offer kindness and compassion to the body. You can use this method of calming the body during periods of mindfulness practice, at various moments in your daily life, or whenever you notice difficulties arising.

Allow the eyes to gently close, and make any adjustments to the body that feel helpful. As you breathe in, reach the spine up. With the exhalation, relax the muscles. Take a few deep breaths like this to arrive in the body, invite in energy, and encourage relaxation.

Rest in awareness of the body for a few moments. You can use the practice of observing points of contact or scanning the body to help yourself settle. Don't force the mind to do anything. Relax into present-time awareness.

Connect with your intention to be calm and at ease. Although there may be tension, anxiety, or discomfort in the body, recognize your own natural wish for the body to be comfortable

Begin o ering a few phrases of loving-kindness to the body. These phrases serve as a way of connecting with our own intentions to care for the body. Try saying them slowly, connecting with the words and their meanings.

You may try o ering a phrase with each exhale. With the intention of cultivating care, o er these phrases:

- May my body be at ease

- May my body be healthy

- May I be at ease with the body

Tune in to speci c parts of the body that grab your attention. Whatever body part comes up, o er a few phrases of loving-kindness.

Open your awareness to any part of the body that is experiencing di culty or pain. Recognizing the discomfort, o er a few phrases of compassion. Compassion is simply attending to pain with a tender and open heart. Try using these phrases

- May my [body part] be free from discomfort.

- May I care about this discomfort

- May I be present for this discomfort.

After a few moments of resting with the discomfort in the body part, open the awareness again. Where else are you feeling discomfort? O er phrases of compassion again here.

Continue with this practice as many times as necessary.

PHRASES AND MANTRAS

The phrases used in meditation serve as a method of tuning in deeply to an intention. They are a type of mantra, a repeated phrase used to aid concentration. If you decide to experiment with them, know that the traditional phrases used in this exercise (and throughout the book) may not feel authentic to you, and that's okay. You can —and should— create a phrase that lands as honest for you and your personal experience. I sometimes say "This stinks" when it's all I can say honestly. I also like

"I love you; keep going." As you practice, rest your awareness on the phrases as you say them silently in your head. If you're in a space where you may do so, you can also try saying the phrases out loud. Experiment with different words to see what feels supportive, caring, and true for you

9
Giving and Receiving

The breath can aid your practice in many different ways, including acting as a vehicle toward peace and acceptance. This practice is called tonglen, a Tibetan word that means "giving and receiving." In this meditation, you work with the breath to help cultivate care and loving-kindness toward yourself and those around you. It is a practice both in mindfulness and compassion. As you move through this exercise, notice any resistance that arises. When the mind wanders, bring it back to the body breathing.

> *"Tonglen practice begins to dissolve the illusion that each of us is alone with this personal suffering that no one else can understand."*

Gently close the eyes and bring your attention to the present moment. Notice where you are. What can you feel in the body? What can you hear? Where are you? There's no need to do anything other than observe your present-time experience in this moment

Bring your awareness to a location in the body where you can feel the breath. For this practice, the chest works well. Be with the body breathing for a minute, feeling the inhalations and exhalations as they come and go

Start the giving and receiving with an intention of self-acceptance. As you breathe in, visualize yourselfbreathing in acceptance. As you exhale, let go of self-judgment. Breathe like this for a few deep breaths.

Begin o ering yourself some ease and peace with each inhale. Let go of stress and anxiety with each exhale. You may try the visualization of breathing in a light of ease, while exhaling the darkness of stress

Now inhale and o er yourself forgiveness. You do not need to go into any stories or rationalizations about this; just set the intention to forgive yourself. As you exhale, let go of resentment

Letting go of the forgiveness and resentment, picture yourself surrounded by people you love. Return to the rst part of working with acceptance and judgment, but this time, ip it around. When inhaling, take in the pain of others as they judge themselves. When exhaling, o er acceptance to your loved ones.

Continue to inhale the stress and anxiety in others, and give ease and peace as you exhale. Hold space for their stress, but don't take it on yourself. By receiving, you're just recognizing with compassion that others have di cult experiences as well

Finally, inhale and tune in to the resentments these people have toward themselves. Exhale and radiate forgiveness for these individuals.

When 10 minutes have passed, allow the eyes to gently open. Let the body resume normal breathing. Remember, you can return to this practice at any point in your day

ADJUST THE PRACTICE: There are multiple ways to utilize this practice. Try choosing di erent di cult experiences and caring qualities to o er. You can also work with whatever arises. If you notice self-judgment arising, use that. Breathe in and recognize that you are experiencing self-judgment. Breathe out and o er the wish that all others are also free from self-judgment. This can help us not get lost in our own su ering or di culty.

10
Body Awareness

The body scan you practiced earlier (Exercise 6, Scanning the Body) is a useful preparation for this exercise. Instead of moving through the body, resting on specific parts, however, this is more of an open awareness that lays the foundation for feeling the emotions in the body and responding with compassion. As with the body scan (or any of these practices), you can return to this anytime.

Find a comfortable meditation posture. You can lie down during this practice, but if you nd yourself growing tired or falling asleep, sit up straight while meditating.

Notice where in the body you can feel the breath. Pick one spot where the sensation of breathing is strongest, and collect the mind onto this part of the body. You may try using a simple mantra of "In, out." For the rst minute or so, give the mind some space to settle into practice.

Expand that awareness to the whole body. From head to toe, acknowledge whenever something grabs your attention. You don't need to seek anything special. Wait patiently with the breath for a feeling in the body to emerge.

When something comes forward, observe what you feel. It may help to use a one-word label, discerning where in the body the sensation is occurring. For example, note "knee" when you feel a pain in the knee or "chest" when you notice the sensation of the breath in the chest. Don't label what the feeling is; label where it is.

Tend to the sensation for a few breaths, and return to the spot in the body where you are focusing on the breath.

Continue to observe the breath until another sensation pops up.

Maintain this practice of alternating between the breath and other sensations in the body. Each time your attention is drawn elsewhere in the body, stay with it for a few moments before returning to the breath. Get to know your body and explore its experiences with curiosity

ADDING TO THE PRACTICE: If you want to add to this practice, start with a body scan prior to step 3 in this exercise. This can relax you and help you get more in tune with your bodily sensations.

PAIN IN THE BODY

If you have consistent pain or discomfort in the body, it may continue to call for your attention. No matter how many times you try to shift your awareness, you are drawn back to this one place of pain. When that happens, listen. Maybe this area needs some loving attention. Try to look at the pain with beginner's mind. Switch to a phrase of self-compassion for your body, even something simple, like "It's okay."

11
Mind Your Steps

Walking meditation is a common practice in many Buddhist traditions, yet it has been largely lost in Western meditation culture. Acclaimed Buddhist teacher Jack Kornfield says, "The art of walking meditation is to learn to be aware as you walk, to use the natural movement of walking to cultivate mindfulness and wakeful presence." Just as you bring awareness to the body that is sitting in meditation, you can bring awareness to a body that is moving.

To practice walking meditation, start by nding about 10 to 15 feet of space. You can walk inside your home, outside in your yard, or anywhere you can access enough distance

Stand still for a moment and close the eyes. Feel the body's posture, the feet on the ground, and any movement you experience.

Open the eyes. Choose which leg will be stepping rst. As you lift the foot, feel the bottom of the foot lose contact with the ground. Moving it forward, observe the sensation of the foot coming back into contact with the ground.

Lift the other foot and attend to the experience with the same awareness. Remember that this is both a mindfulness practice and a practice in cultivating concentration. When the mind wanders, come back to the feeling in the feet.

Walk 10 or 15 feet, and mindfully turn around. As you turn, notice how the hips, legs, and torso adjust to turn the body. Walk slowly, taking a step every three or four seconds.

You may try incorporating a simple verbal noticing practice, similar to a mantra. As you lift the foot, think (or say), "Lift." As you move the foot forward, think, "Move." As you place the foot down, think, "Place."

When you are done with the period of practice, stand still for a few moments. Moving out of the period of meditation and back into daily life, you can retain some of this mindfulness of the body

12
Caring for Yourself

The practice of metta, or loving-kindness, can help you respond to your own mind with friendliness. Unfortunately, our thoughts don't always do what we want them to, and the body may have discomfort. Loving-kindness meditation encourages us to meet those experiences with a caring and gentle heart. This helps us see more clearly in our practice and daily life. In loving-kindness practice, you are not inviting in something from outside yourself; you are tuning in to the capacity for care and love that is already present in your heart.

> *"Your task is not to seek for love, but merely to seek and find all the barriers within yourself that you have built against it."*

Sit in a comfortable posture and gently allow the eyes to close. From the beginning, try to bring kindness to the practice. Think of the body with friendliness. Listen to it and see if you can move to get more comfortable. You don't want to fall asleep, but you can allow yourself to be more at ease during this exercise

Begin by recognizing your own desire to be happy. Don't dig into stories about what might make you happy. Find this natural wish for ease and comfort for yourself. Try saying to yourself, "Yes, I want to be happy."

With this intention in mind, begin o ering yourself phrases of loving-kindness. As you o er the phrases in your head, say them slowly. Connect with the intention behind the words, even if you don't feel them entirely in this moment. Use these phrases:

◆ May I be happy

- ◆ May I be healthy

- ◆ May I be safe.

- ◆ May I be at ease

Find a rhythm with the phrases. You may try o ering one phrase with each exhale or with every other exhale. As you o er the phrases, use them as the object of your concentration. Rest your awareness fully on the phrases and the deeper intention.

When the mind wanders, come back to the phrases in your head. Notice any feelings or thoughts of self-judgment or resistance to self-care.

Stay with the phrases for as long as you feel comfortable. I recommend starting with 10 minutes.

NOT FEELING IT

You may not really "feel it" while cultivating kindness for yourself. In other moments, you may have overwhelming feelings of love and care. Release any judgment and continue to open the heart. This is a practice that helps us cultivate a quality. If the quality of kindness is not present in your meditation session, know that you are taking action to create this caring feeling in the future.

13
Unhooking from Thoughts

Thoughts are part of everyone's human experience. You don't need to push them away in order to practice—learning to bring your mind back from its thoughts is the practice. But how do you let go of the thoughts once they've pulled you in? This exercise offers one way to "unhook" yourself from those thoughts and simply let them be. Without pushing the thoughts away or denying their presence, you can be aware of the thinking mind while remaining unattached

Settle into a seated posture and close the eyes. Notice the energy in the mind and body. As you come into a period of mindfulness practice, you may notice the energy of your day resting in the mind and body. The mind may be active, the body may feel worked up, or you might notice a bit of lingering anxiety.

Think of a shaken snow globe, with all that energy swirling around. As you rest, the little snow akes fall gently to the ground. Think of yourself as a snow globe, and every snow ake as a thought. In this way, watch as each and every snow ake falls to the ground. Do not force yourself to calm down; let it happen slowly and organically.

After a minute or so, bring your attention to the breath in the body. Choose one spot where the breath is felt easily. It may be the center of the chest, the abdomen, the shoulders, or the nostrils. Observe the physical sensation of the body breathing. You may use the counting practice from Exercise 7, Every Breath Counts, if you nd it helpful.

Observing the breath for a few minutes, bring the mind back when it wanders. Stick with the snow globe visualization, and as thoughts begin to rise up, observe as they slowly settle back down.

After a couple of minutes of focusing on the breath, open your awareness to include your thoughts and your general mental state. Instead of returning to the breath when the mind wanders, notice what the mind is doing. You may notice yourself planning, fantasizing, " guring out," or replaying past experiences. Whatever you observe the mind doing, let it be.

When you recognize a thought, what happens? Try not to encourage the thought, but don't push it away, either. Allow it to be, and allow it to go on its own. See if you can watch the passing of the thought as it follows its natural trajectory and leaves the mind

Return to the breath and patiently wait until another thought arises. Notice it, watch the thought, and come back to the breath again. Continue with mindfulness of the breath and the thoughts

Notice when you're lost in thought or when the mind wanders for some time. If self-judgment arises, notice that just as you would any other thought. You can always return to the breath for a few moments to ground yourself back into the practice

MINDING YOUR MENTAL STATE: Notice your mental states when they arise. If the mind grows anxious or frustrated, acknowledge that it has done so. Mental states like these may be present with or without concrete thoughts arising

SEDUCTIVE AND TRICKY THOUGHTS

The thinking mind can be cunning and seductive, and certain thoughts (or patterns of thought) have

the power to pull us in immediately.

 Although you may be able to "unhook" from certain thoughts with ease, others may be too powerful. Recognize these patterns and what types of thoughts continually control your awareness. When you find yourself grasped by one of these thoughts, smile at the trickster mind and just keep trying.

14
Energizing the Mind

During meditation practice, the mind can grow dull or sleepy. In this short practice, you will examine a few ways to bring energy and alertness to your mind. You can incorporate these methods into your other practices, inviting clarity into your meditation

Allow the eyes to close, and nd a comfortable meditation posture. Begin by tuning in to the experience of the body breathing. Rest with each inhale and exhale as you feel the movement in the body.

To energize the mind, you will start with the breath. With the inhalation, breathe in a sense of energy and awareness. Reach the body upward, straighten the spine, and open the chest. With the exhale, let go of sleepiness and distraction.

After a minute or two, allow the eyes to open—letting light in can help us stay awake and clear. Continue practicing with the breath and notice any sights that grab your attention.

Allow a few minutes to pass, and stand up. With your eyes open, standing on your feet, you are inviting increased alertness into your practice. It's much harder to fall asleep standing up than sitting down

As you complete this exercise, take a moment to shake out your body and get some energy moving. Feel the warmth in your muscles as you move and go back to your day.

RESISTING SLEEPINESS

During formal meditation, you may notice the mind growing sleepy. Practices like this one can be woven into your daily practice to help induce a more wakeful state of mind. If you notice sleepiness arising, do not deny that it is present. Recognize that your mind is tired, and try to refrain from judgment. Also know that the more opportunities you give the mind to rest in stillness, the less sleepy you'll become over time.

15
The Attitude of Gratitude

This exercise comes from the Buddhist practice of mudita, which means "appreciative joy." It can be understood as simply "showing up" for happiness with a caring presence. As you train the mind to rejoice in happiness, you gain many benefits. You feel more fulfilled by joy, recognize happiness more easily in your life, and train the mind to treat happiness as an important experience

> *"Every time you take in the good, you build a little bit of neural structure. Doing this a few times a day—for months and even years—will gradually change your brain, and how you feel and act, in far-reaching ways."*

Find a comfortable posture and invite in relaxation from the beginning of your practice. As you breathe, appreciate the life o ered from each inhalation. With the exhalation, let go of any tension in the mind or body.

Bring to mind a time in which you recently experienced happiness. It may be something small, like seeing a friend, watching the sunset, or the simple joy of lying down at night. When you have something, allow yourself to feel the experience of contentment.

With the intention of cultivating gratitude, o er yourself a few phrases of appreciative joy. Keep the memory in your mind, and o er these phrases:

- May my happiness continue

- May my happiness grow

- May I be present for the joy

- May I appreciate the joy in my life.

If your experience feels more like contentment or ease, you can substitute the words that resonate with you. You know your own experience, so be true to yourself

Other the phrases silently in your head, nding a rhythm with the practice. Focus your attention on the words, the intention of appreciating the happiness, and the feeling of contentment from your memory.

After ve minutes, release the memory and the phrases from your mind. Bring to mind somebody else in your life who has experienced some happiness recently

Picture this person in your mind, smiling as you observe their joy

As you did with yourself, o er phrases of gratitude. Rejoice as much as possible in their happiness. O er these phrases:

- May your happiness continue

- May your happiness grow

- May I be present for your joy.

- I'm happy for you.

When the mind wanders, come back to the phrases. You can return to the visualization of this person smiling to bring up the happiness, and start with the phrases again. Continue this for ve minutes.

WHY GRATITUDE MATTERS

In our daily lives, we often do not truly appreciate the moments of contentment, whether they're small or significant. Instead, the brain latches onto the difficult and painful moments, or becomes obsessed with solving problems. With this appreciative -joy practice, you can retrain the mind to give weight to your pleasant experiences, however small. By continuing to practice gratitude, you'll notice happiness more often in your life.

16
Resting the Mind

Throughout these exercises and during your daily routine, you may notice the mind growing restless or agitated. Although you cannot always control the mind, you can encourage it to be more at ease. Learning to do this will help you respond rather than react to your thoughts and emotions. This practice gives you the opportunity to train the mind to slow down when it becomes overactive, and helps you practice ease and relaxation instead of perpetuating those difficult mental states.

You can sit upright or lie down for this practice. If you are experiencing anxiety or stress in this moment, lying down may encourage relaxation.

Take a few deep breaths. Inhaling, ll the lungs completely. Hold the breath for just a second or two, and exhale slowly. As you let the breath go, try to empty the lungs slowly and completely

Recognizing that you cannot control every thought that arises, connect with your intention to relax the mind. If thoughts are present, just leave them be. O er yourself two simple phrases of kindness toward the mind:

- ◆ May my mind be at ease.

- ◆ May I be at ease with my mind

Synchronize these phrases with your exhale, o ering one phrase every time you breathe out. Hear each word and try to connect with your own intention to care for the mind.

When the thinking mind starts up, come back to the breath and the phrases. Even if you can say only one phrase before the mind wanders, you are still moving toward relaxation by continuing to practice.

Completing this exercise, allow the eyes to open, and return to the activity of daily life. Watch the mind during your day, noticing when it becomes uncomfortable or agitated

SWITCHING TO COMPASSION: The mind and its thoughts can become painful in certain moments. You may experience guilt, anxiety, or grief. In these times, the above phrases may not be appropriate. Switch instead to mantras of compassion. Recognize that it hurts, and tend to your pain with care. Try this simple sentiment: "May I care for this pain."

THE STUBBORN MIND

Sometimes, the mind just won't settle down. The harder you strain, the more agitated it grows. If your mind is overactive and won't slow down, try instead to change your response to that experience. Instead of stressing to calm the mind, focus your energy on accepting that the mind is working overtime and on responding with compassion

17
The Judgment-Free Zone

The practice of noting is a foundational aspect of mindfulness. Popular in MBSR and insight meditation, noting allows us to clearly observe what is happening without getting hooked into the experience. This "nonjudgmental noting" exercise will help you practice separating your judgment of your experiences from the experiences themselves. When you begin to untangle the two, you start training your mind to let go.

Sit in an upright position and let the eyes close. Using the breath, invite both awareness and relaxation into the body and mind. Breathing in, reach the spine upward and bring energy into the body. Breathing out, let everything go. Let the jaw go slack, drop the shoulders away from the ears, and soften the muscles of the belly.

Start opening your awareness to include any sensations in the body. Following the instructions in Exercise 10, Body Awareness, note where in the body a feeling is present. Mindfully observe that feeling for a few moments; then open yourself up to other experiences in the body.

After settling into this practice for a few minutes, notice when the mind begins judging. The mind may label some experiences or feelings as good or right, and others as bad or wrong. Don't encourage or discourage these judgments; just notice them when they come up. Continue like this for a few minutes.

Invite the sense of hearing into your practice. When you hear a sound, recognize that you are hearing. If a judgment arises about the sound, recognize it but don't try to do anything about it.

Continue practicing with openness. Whether you are hearing, feeling something in the body, or hooked into a thought, remain aware of your experience. Whenever a judgment is present, name it and leave it be. Resist the tendency to push it away, but do not engage with it any further.

Finish with a few deep breaths, settling the awareness back into the body before opening the eyes.

> **JUDGING YOURSELF FOR JUDGING**
>
> **With this practice, you are tuning directly in to your judgments. The moment you see judgment arising, you may habitually respond by judging yourself for having the judgment. (It's that trickster mind at work again!) One of the most useful things you can do when this happens is to laugh at yourself. The mind is a funny thing. Try not to take yourself so seriously.**

18
The Four Elements

This practice dates back over 2,500 years and provides a different lens through which you can examine the body. Because this practice may feel awkward at first, try to take some extra time with it. Give yourself space to drop in and deeply investigate these elements in your body. Try to bring an open mind, and see what you can learn about yourself. Remember that mindfulness is about seeing clearly, and looking at things from a new perspective can often bring that clarity

Settle into a relaxed position. Close the eyes, and bring your awareness to the places in the body where you experience contact, such as the feet on the oor, the hands in the lap, or the body sitting in the chair.

Begin with the element of earth or solid form. Without thinking too hard about what this means, openly examine where and how you can feel solidity. This might be the structure of your skeleton, the chair you're sitting on, any places of tension in the body, or the weight of your muscles as they relax. Don't rush through these sensations or try to force them. When you feel the earth element in the body, stay with it for a few deep breaths. Continue this seeking, recognizing, and feeling for a few breaths.

After ve minutes, switch to the element of air or wind. An obvious place to start is in the form of the body breathing. Where can you feel the air of the breath? You may also look for places in the body where you can feel empty space—the nostrils, the mouth, and the ears can o er insight into the air element.

When another ve minutes have passed, shift your awareness to the water element. Tune in to any sense of liquidity you can feel. There may be moisture in the eyes, saliva in the mouth, or sweat on the body—or you can feel the exibility of your muscles, the ow of your breath in and out, or even the pulsing of your blood.

Next, bring your attention to heat or re in the body. This element is open to interpretation, so look for yourself to see what you notice. Perhaps it's the temperature of the air touching your skin, or certain spots on the body that are warmer or cooler than others. Watch for any experience of temperature, either externally or internally.

To wrap up the practice, spend a few moments in awareness of the body as a whole. As you breathe, feel the four elements working together to support and fuel your body.

CREATING A QUICK FOUR-ELEMENTS PRACTICE

To create a quicker practice from this exercise, pick one of the four elements to focus on. If you've been feeling especially anxious and scattered, the earth element can help ground you. If you're feeling stuck or stubborn, air or water will help loosen things up. And if you've experienced any situation where you feel powerless, try connecting to the fire inside.
This practice also works as an active meditation to use throughout the day. Connect to the air element through the breath or the breeze. While walking, notice the element of heat as the movement warms you up. All four elements are always present in our bodies and in the world at large. Give yourself the freedom to explore different ways of identifying and experiencing them.

19
Tuning In to Feeling Tones

Whenever an experience comes into your awareness, you can look at it more deeply by acknowledging its feeling tone. Feeling tones are not emotions. A feeling tone describes what you're experiencing as pleasant, unpleasant, or neutral. A feeling tone can be attached to anything you perceive through the senses, including a thought. By noticing the feeling tone, you continue to deepen your insight into the nature of your experience.

Settle into a comfortable sitting posture. As you allow the eyes to close, focus on the sensations of the body breathing. You may use the counting exercise (Exercise 7, Every Breath Counts) to focus the mind. Concentrate on the breath for the rst few minutes, dropping into a state of grounded mindfulness.

Include the whole body in your awareness. As you did in Exercise 10, Body Awareness, spend a few minutes just noticing what arises in the body. Don't judge anything as good or bad; just pay attention to the actual experience of feeling in the body

Once you are present with the bodily sensations, expand your awareness to include feeling tones. Acknowledge the feeling in the body, and consider whether the experience is pleasant, unpleasant, or neutral. If you like, you can do a body scan (Exercise 6, Scanning the Body) and notice the feeling tone for each place in the body.

Once you are present with the bodily sensations, expand your awareness to include feeling tones. Acknowledge the feeling in the body, and consider whether the experience is pleasant, unpleasant, or neutral. If you like, you can do a body scan (Exercise 6, Scanning the Body) and notice the feeling tone for each place in the body.

Finally, include the thoughts. You don't need to dive into exactly what you're thinking—recognize when a thought is present and if there is a feeling tone attached. Then open back up and wait for the next experience to arise.

Resting in open mindfulness can leave space for mental wandering. Remember that you can always return to the breath as your anchor during this practice. Don't hesitate to return to it for a minute or two in order to collect the mind.

Take a few deep breaths and open the eyes. Moving through your day, see if you can notice feeling tones attached to what you see, hear, and feel.

BE OPEN TO CHANGE: Feeling tones are not stable or xed. In one moment you may nd an experience to be pleasant, and in the next it may feel unpleasant. Remember to practice beginner's mind, remaining curious and open.

NOT KNOWING

Some experiences may not have a clear feeling tone. Although we generally work with pleasant, unpleasant, or neutral, there are other options you can play with, as well. If you do not know the feeling tone, say, "I don't know." If it feels mixed, say, "Mixed." There's no use in straining if the feeling tone is not clear. Be honest, honoring your own personal experience.

20
The Emotional Experience

Emotions are complex occurrences that can be most simply understood as a combination of physical sensations and thought patterns. When you mindfully tune in to your emotional experience, you can begin to break it down and separate yourself from its power. With wisdom and care, you'll become able to let go of your feelings rather than allowing them to rule you.

> **"You have a unique body and mind, with a particular history and conditioning. No one can offer you a formula for navigating all situations and all states of mind. Only by listening inwardly in a fresh and open way will you discern at any given time what most serves your healing and freedom."**

Find a posture that feels both comfortable and conducive to mindfulness. Although you may know what works for you in general, be open to any adjustments that can be made. Take a few moments to examine the body and what is present.

Bring to mind a recent experience of joy or happiness. Try to recall as many details as you can about this event. Visualize the experience, and give it space to be present in the mind and body

As this emotional experience is with you, investigate it closely. What is this joy? Notice what you feel in the body. You may notice a relaxing of the shoulders, gentler or deeper breaths, or a warmth in the chest.

There's nothing you should or should not be feeling; just recognize your own experience of joy.

Tune in to the mental state that accompanies this physical sensation. As you rest with the memory of joy, what is happening in the mind? Notice if it is calm, active, agitated, or at ease. There isn't a right or wrong answer. Familiarize yourself with the experience of joy.

Now, do the same with a recent experience that was unpleasant. It may be a time in which you were stressed, anxious, frustrated, or sad. Steer clear of experiences that are powerfully charged, like an intense argument or workplace conflict. Instead, start with something minorly unpleasant, like sitting in traffic or navigating a crowded grocery store.

Investigate this experience in both mind and body, resting with each for a few minutes.

Return to the body and the breath for a minute at the end of your practice. Allow the mind to relax for a few deep breaths before opening the eyes.

WORKING WITH OPEN EMOTIONS

Instead of intentionally calling up past emotions, you can do this practice with open awareness and work with any emotion arising as you sit. If you patiently wait with mindfulness, you have an opportunity to observe how emotions come and go. Recognizing the transient nature of your feelings can help you become less attached to them over time. You may also pause to do this during your day whenever you notice yourself having an emotional experience.

21
Grounded and Flexible

Equanimity is the quality of remaining grounded and stable in the midst of your experience. When you notice suffering, you respond with compassion, and you don't get knocked off balance by the unexpected. With equanimity practice, you cultivate a state of mind that is both grounded and flexible, especially in the midst of intense emotional experiences.

> *"A modern definition of equanimity: cool. This refers to one whose mind remains stable and calm in all situations."*

Closing the eyes and nding your posture, bring your awareness into your present experience. Notice the sounds, the feelings in the body, and your overall mental state.

Open your awareness. When something comes up, tune in to the mind, noticing where you get knocked o balance. Certain sounds, thoughts, or feelings in the body may feel charged, pulling you from your calm state of mind. Sit with this awareness of your own balance for ve minutes.

Bring to mind someone you care about deeply. Connect with your intention to care for this person. Recognize that although you may care for this person, you cannot control their happiness. Other a few phrases of equanimity:

- May you be happy.

- Your happiness is dependent upon your actions, not my wishes for you

◆ May you be in charge of your happiness

After five minutes, switch to somebody else you care about. Try to find someone who is currently experiencing some pain or suffering. Connecting with your intention to care but remain stable, offer these phrases of compassion and equanimity:

◆ May you be free from suffering

◆ May you take action to care for your pain.

◆ Your freedom is dependent upon your actions, not my wishes for you.

Finally, bring to mind somebody in your life who has had some joy or success recently. Offer a few phrases of appreciative joy, staying connected to your equanimity.

◆ May your joy continue.

◆ May you be in charge of your joy

◆ Your joy is in your hands and is not dependent upon my wishes for you.

After a few minutes of offering these phrases, return to your own experience before opening the eyes. Recognize that your happiness is in your own hands. Be proud of your effort in practicing, encouraging happiness for yourself.

FALLING INTO APATHY

Equanimity has what is called a "near enemy." This is a quality that looks similar but is actually not helpful. The near enemy of equanimity is apathy — the quality of not caring at all. Whereas equanimity is about attending to your experience with care and stability, apathy is turning away from the ex-

perience altogether and ceasing to care. Watch out for apathy or indifference as you practice. If apathy arises, return to your phrases of loving-kindness, reconnecting with the naturally caring part of your heart.

22
Feel the Love

This practice offers an alternate way to allow ourselves to be cared for. We will work with a technique of visualization in receiving love and care. This will help you cultivate the capacity to accept love and recognize your innate worthiness.

As you nd a comfortable posture and allow the eyes to close, make a special e ort to bring kindness to your practice today. Relax the body and let the mind be at ease.

Bring to mind a person who cares for you. It may be a family member, a good friend, or a mentor of some kind. Picture this person standing in front of you, o ering you phrases of loving-kindness. Your job is simply to receive their wishes. Continue receiving these intentions for ve minutes.

Add another person who cares about you into the mix. Accept the wishes of well-being from these two individuals, allowing their care and love to land deeply in your consciousness.

After a few minutes, bring in a third individual. Continue bringing others in slowly until you have a group of people in front of you, o ering you words and feelings of kindness. Try to accept these wishes with an open heart.

When you come to the end of your practice, bring your own gentleness and care into your experience. Open the eyes slowly, and make your way back into daily life with patient kindness

CLOSING THE HEART

The heart and mind can grow uncomfortable as they receive love. You may not feel worthy of the love or kindness you are receiving. Notice when and if the heart begins closing, or when the mind tries to distract you with stories. Try to tune back in to the felt sense of receiving love in the body. Work toward achieving an embodied sense of being loved.

23
Cultivating Concentration

In Exercise 7, Every Breath Counts, you used breath counting to help build concentration in the mind for a short period of time. Dedicating longer intervals to this practice can help you deepen your mindfulness practice (and it's useful in day-to-day life as well). Starting with the counting of the breath, this exercise offers a few different ways to build concentration more deeply.

After you settle into your posture, begin with the practice of counting the breaths. Focus the attention on the body breathing, and bring the mind back every time it wanders. Practice like this for the rst ve minutes.

Let go of the counting, but stay with the breath. Mindfully watch the breath with your full awareness, noticing if it becomes more di cult without the counting. Continue for ve minutes.

Now, switch to the sensation of hearing. Find a relatively stable noise in your environment. It may be the sound of a nearby street, the humming of electricity or lights, or the subtle ringing in the ears. Use your hearing as the object of your awareness. When the mind wanders, come back to this sound

After ve minutes, open the eyes. Find one object on which you can focus your attention. Look at it with curiosity, noticing every detail of the object—its outline, its color, its texture, and so on. When other sights, sounds, or thoughts distract you, return to the object you have chosen. Practice this for the nal ve minutes.

MONKEY MIND

When working with concentration, you may experience what's called "monkey mind." Monkey mind is when the mind is unsettled, jumping around like a monkey swinging from tree to tree. If monkey mind becomes distracting, open yourself up to the thoughts. Although you may start this exercise with the intention of building concentration, give yourself permission to switch to a mindfulness-of-thoughts practice. Recognize the thoughts arising, welcome them in, and don't push them away.

24
Open-Awareness Meditation

This is a traditional mindfulness meditation, similar to what most people think of when they hear the word meditation. Using mindfulness of the senses, feeling tones, and your overall experience in the present moment, this is a practice in true open awareness. It is the cornerstone of mindfulness practice for many meditators across the world.

Open-Awareness Meditation is a combination of some of the shorter, more focused exercises earlier in this section. Throughout the exercise, rest in openness, receiving whatever arises into your experience.

Start with a brief body scan. Moving from head to toe, rest your attention on each part of the body with mindfulness.

After completing the body scan, open your awareness to the sensations in the body—tension, pain, softness, the desire to dget, or maybe an emotion or feeling. What arises and grabs your attention? Mindfully observe the body for ve minutes.

Open your practice to the experience of hearing. When a sound comes into your awareness, acknowledge that you are hearing. Sit for ve minutes with patience, noticing any bodily sensations or sounds present.

Continue to open, this time including the thinking mind. You may see thoughts, emotional experiences, or general mental states. Whatever is present, note that you are having an experience of the mind.

Finally, add in the practice of noting feeling tone. Cultivate an intention to receive and remain open. Recognize whatever is present in your awareness and how it feels. If the mind is reacting to any part of your experience, make that reaction a part of your practice.

As you complete this meditation and move into daily life, try to sustain some of this awareness. OPEN MINDFULNESS DURING YOUR DAY: You can make this practice a part of your everyday mindfulness. Pause for a few moments during your day and start with the fth step of this exercise. Open up to your entire experience, and spend a minute or two noting what is present. This can help bring you back to the present-time experience in stressful or boring moments

TOO OPEN

Open-mindfulness practice can sometimes feel too open. By allowing space for anything to arise, you may start to feel lazy or overly relaxed. As the mind relaxes, it may start to spin out on random trains of thought. If you find this happening, try tightening your awareness a bit by focusing on one of your five senses (hearing usually works well). Remember that every time you bring the mind back, you are strengthening the mental muscles of mindfulness and concentration.

25
Breathing and Noting

This is an alternate way to work with open mindfulness, and it's how I practice every day. This combination of intentional concentration and open awareness is inspired by the Burmese monk Mahasi Sayadaw. Breathing and Noting is a popular practice among students of mindfulness across the world.

> *"Every time one notes an object well, it gives rise to delight. As a result of this, practice becomes enjoyable."*

Settle the body into a comfortable posture and allow the eyes to close. Focus your awareness on the breath. You can start with a counting exercise if you nd it helpful. Choosing one location in the body, use the simple terms in and out to note each inhale and exhale. Continue for ve minutes or more, until the mind begins to settle. Staying with the inhale and exhale, bring your awareness to the body in general. After the exhale, note one place in the body where you can feel a sensation. For example, you may note the following: "In, out, foot"; "In, out, chest"; and so on.

After ve minutes, incorporate the sensation of hearing. Continue to note the inhalation and exhalation; then note a feeling in the body or a sound. Next, open up to the thinking mind. As you have been doing, continue resting with the breath. As you breathe out, open up to any thoughts, feelings in the body, and sounds.

Finally, include feeling tones. You now are resting with the breath and noting any bodily sensations, noises, thoughts, and feeling tones after each exhale.

ANXIETY AND FEELING OVERWHELMED

You may notice feeling overwhelmed or stress arising during this practice. Welcome it in and make it a part of your practice. You can try slowing the breath down to encourage relaxation, or return to the simple practice of breath counting to give yourself a break before opening the awareness back up.

26
The Awareness Trigger

One of the most difficult parts about practicing mindfulness is actually remembering to practice. For this reason, an awareness trigger can help you form a habit. You can incorporate this at multiple points throughout your day, experiment with different triggers, and use different methods of mindfulness with this exercise.

In the morning, pick one task or event that is likely to happen a few times during the day, for example, the sound of the phone ringing, the act of sitting down, or seeing the color red.

Picking one event or behavior, set a clear intention to use this as a trigger for mindfulness throughout your day. Take a moment to connect with your goals and hopes for yourself, encouraging awareness during your day.

Whenever you notice your trigger, pause and practice a few moments of mindfulness. You can do any of the exercises from part 1—working with the breath, observing the points of contact, or any other method in this book that works for you

After dedicating a few moments to present-time awareness, you can return to your daily life. Remember to continue bringing awareness to the present moment whenever your trigger arises throughout the day

FINDING THE RIGHT TRIGGER: There are many di er-ent triggers you can use for this practice. Give yourself the freedom to choose a trigger that's relevant and reliable in your lifestyle. If you work in front of a computer, you may try using the receipt of an e-mail.

27
Waking Up with Awareness

One of the best techniques to help bring mindfulness to everyday living is to start your day with it. Many of us have a rushed morning routine and do not pause to be present until later in the day. This exercise can help you start off your day with a mindful moment, bolstering your practice in the coming hours.

When you wake up, take a moment to pause before you get up. If you use an alarm clock, try attaching a sticky note to it to remind yourself.

Lying in bed, tune in to the body. Feel the body resting, and notice how it feels to begin moving and stretching

Bring your awareness to the breath. Taking a few deep breaths, recognize that you woke up and are breathing this morning.

As you get up and begin your day, try to retain some awareness. Routines make it easy to fall into autopilot. Notice when you lose your presence, and come back to mindfulness.

THE MORNING CHAOS

Mornings may be an especially chaotic time. Rushing to get to work, taking care of children, and dealing with the foggy morning brain can make it difficult to really be present. This calls for extra effort and kindness. The places and times that give you trouble are often the richest opportunities to practice. Notice when your mind and body are moving toward stress. You don't need to do anything; watch

it happen with patient awareness. Just observing this process can help you understand it more deeply and become less vulnerable to it in the future

28
The Creative Flow

Taking the time to be creative during your day can build lasting benefits in all areas of your life. Creativity can boost self-awareness, relieve stress, and help you solve problems more easily. In addition, you can cultivate mindfulness while indulging your creative side. Do this exercise with your activity of choice, and remember that you can pause at any time and use this technique to encourage present-time awareness.

Get a blank piece of paper and a pen. If you want to use crayons, markers, or colored pencils, that is even better. Set aside 10 minutes, perhaps setting a timer if it helps you really dedicate the time to practice.

Bring your awareness to your experience in this moment. Feel the pen in the hand, see the piece of paper, and notice any thoughts going through the mind. If judgment arises about your creative talents, notice them as they come up.

Start drawing. You don't need to create a masterpiece. There is nothing wrong with stick gures and doodles. Draw whatever you want. It may be a happy memory, scenery, or something you can see right now

As you draw, notice what you are drawing. If it's a person, note that you're drawing a person. If there is movement, notice there is movement. Watch for any emotions that arise, exploring whether the piece is happy, sad, fun, beautiful, and so on.

Take special care to watch for judgments. However creative you consider yourself to be, you may nd the mind telling you that you're no good. Thank the mind for these contributions and continue drawing.

After 10 minutes, put down the pen. Look at what you've drawn, and take it in. Examine the lines, gures, and overall piece. Again, notice the thoughts and judgments when they arise. You may choose to save the piece, or not—the activity is the point, not the result

CREATIVE OUTLETS: This exercise will work with any form of creativity. Try lling in a coloring book, taking photos, playing an instrument, or dancing. The only limits are the ones you put on yourself! Allow yourself just 10 minutes of freedom from judgment, and follow your passion.

29
Cooking with Clarity

Cooking or preparing a meal is an opportunity to form a loving connection with your food. As you prepare a meal, you can cultivate mindfulness of your body and mind as well as the food you will be eating. Whether you're making a quick meal or preparing a feast, use this exercise to ground yourself in the present moment.

> *"Cooking is at once child's play and adult joy. And cooking done with care is an act of love."*

Start your practice before you start grabbing supplies out of the refrigerator or cabinet. Form an image in your mind of the meal you will be preparing. Envision both the completed meal and the individual ingredients. Notice your intentions in preparing this meal.

As you begin gathering the things you will need, tune in to the body. Feel the body moving across the kitchen and reaching for each item. To help cultivate mindfulness, make an e ort to move more slowly than you normally do.

As you chop, stir, and prepare, focus on one thing at a time. When turning on the stove, don't just turn the stove on. Feel the experience with your complete awareness. Whatever you are doing, bring your attention wholly to the task in front of you.

Use your senses. Notice if you're hearing, feeling in the body, tasting, smelling, or seeing. When you see water boiling, investigate the sight, the feeling of heat, and the sound. As you chop vegetables, listen to the noise of the knife, feel the utensil in your hand, and notice if you can smell anything. Using all ve senses helps you remain present and interested

When the meal is complete, pause to appreciate the experience. Recognize the e ort you have put in. Bring gratitude to the energy that went into bringing the food to your kitchen in the rst place. If you're feeding others, re ect that you are providing sustenance to these loved ones. Allow yourself to feel grateful.

30
Mindful Speech

Humans are social creatures. Rarely does a day go by where you don't interact with anyone—maybe you have a family, live with a roommate, or engage with people during work hours. When you talk, you can bring mindfulness to what you are saying, how it may impact others, and what your intentions are. This exercise takes just a few minutes, and you can utilize it anytime. Do this once or twice a day while on the phone, talking with a loved one, or during any social interaction.

Before speaking, bring mindfulness to your intentions. Ask yourself why you are going to say whatever you plan on saying. Examine the possibility of saying it with even more kindness or patience.

Consider whether your words are timely and useful in this moment. We often gossip, interrupt, or talk simply to avoid uncomfortable silences. Think about whether or not this is the appropriate time to talk and what purpose your words will serve.

If it's possible that your words will put somebody else down, interrupt a person currently speaking, or ring as untrue, try reconsidering your choice of words.

While talking, speak slowly and be mindful of the words you are using. When somebody responds either verbally or with body language, observe how it feels. Remember that you cannot control others, but you can bring mindfulness to your own responses

When you are done talking, leave the words be. Listen to the other person and wait for the right time to talk again. As you practice mindful speech more regularly, you will be able to navigate challenging conversations with more ease

RECOGNIZING UNWISE SPEECH: You will likely notice times in which you speak without mindfulness. Set the goal to tune in to your habits of talking. If you nd yourself gossiping a lot, create an intention to avoid gossip. If you interrupt others often, bring special awareness to this pattern. Don't beat yourself up. These are growing edges, and you have the opportunity to attend to them with compassion and kindness.

31
Doing the Dishes

On meditation retreats, I wash dozens of dishes silently every day. It took me years of silent retreats to appreciate this act as an opportunity to be mindful. For most of us, it seems like a dreaded chore. We wash the dishes in haste, rushing to get it done as quickly as possible. Instead, you can partake in this chore with present-time awareness and find some peace.

Look at the dishes you are going to be cleaning. Notice any natural reactions you have to the task at hand. Try to bring to mind the meal that was consumed and how it supported the well-being and life of all those who ate.

Take a few deep breaths, centering your awareness in the body. Feel where you are standing and the weight pushing down the spine into the feet.

Begin to wash, one dish at a time. Stay focused on the dish directly in front of you in the moment. As you clean, tune in to the smells that arise of the soap and food. Watch the dishes become cleaner. Feel the warm water on your hands. Hear the sounds of the water and the scrubbing.

Place the dish in your drying rack or dishwasher slowly, bringing awareness to the body as you do so.

Moving to the next dish, recognize that this is a new start. Let go of the dishes you have cleaned and the dishes still to be cleaned. Return to the one item you are cleaning right now.

Watch the mind wander. When it meanders, bring it back to the task at hand.

32
Mindful Cleaning

Like doing dishes, cleaning grants us the time to step back from our active days and rest in present-time awareness. Instead of focusing on the task itself or how you feel about it (most of us are usually not that excited to clean the house), use this time as a chance to take care of yourself and encourage the habit of mindfulness.

In this exercise, we will use the activity of sweeping. However, you can practice mindful cleaning while dusting, mopping, wiping down a counter, or doing any other household chore.

Start your practice when you are gathering your cleaning supplies. Walking to get the broom, feel the feet moving across the oor. Pay attention to the feeling of moving through space toward your supplies.

Picking up the broom, bring awareness to the sense of touch. If the mind begins wandering into the future and the task at hand, bring yourself back to the body in the present moment.

Sweeping is often repetitive, which can lead to a sense of boredom. To help stay in the present moment, try using a mantra. You can use a simple noting phrase, like "Left, right," or a phrase of loving-kindness, such as "May I live with ease." With each movement of the broom, mentally repeat the phrase in unison with the action.

Recognize any mental states that arise. If you are frustrated, notice that you are frustrated. If curiosity arises about some dirt, recognize that you are curious

Continuing to clean, remember to check in with the body and state of mind. Notice the movements, the repetition, and the emotions that arise. Return to your mantra or phrase as many times as necessary.

When you are nished cleaning, stand still and take a deep breath. Observe the space you have cleaned, and recognize its representation of your clean mind!

33
Journaling

A regular journaling practice is a lovely way to check in with yourself. Dedicate a few minutes each day to examining your experience through writing. This exercise is best to do in the morning and at night in order to start and end your day with mindfulness. It also is useful to have a dedicated journal or notebook for this practice.

Set aside ve minutes in the morning to sit down and journal. As you sit down to do this exercise, tune in to the body sitting in the chair. Feel yourself sitting, the feet on the oor, and the pen or pencil in the hand.

Take a few deep breaths, grounding yourself in the present moment. Recognize the state of the mind this morning. Is it calm, anxious, fearful, or hopeful? You don't need to x anything; just notice where the mind is today.

For a few minutes, mindfully write about your current experience and the day ahead. You may set a timer if this feels like a daunting task. Address how you feel this morning, your state of mind, and any intentions you have for the day. Ask yourself if you have any worries, hopes, or events on the mind

Finishing your journaling practice, return to the breath for a few moments before moving on with your day.

At night, return to this practice. For ve minutes, re ect on your day. Identify anything you are grateful for, re ect on things that you could have handled better, and note any points of mindfulness during your day.

THE MEDITATION JOURNAL

You can also incorporate journaling into your meditation practice. After you sit in traditional meditation, open your journal and put down your experience in writing. Note whether the mind was focused or wandering, how it felt to practice, and anything unique or interesting about that day's practice. Writing about your practice provides extra space for you to look at your experience with curiosity and equanimity.

34
The Moving World

The very nature of mindfulness is to tune in to your experience at any given moment, noticing as you go that every experience is impermanent. That is to say, everything is always changing. Feelings come and go, thoughts arise and pass, and sounds pop up and disappear. We can use this changing nature as the object of our awareness during the day. Tuning in to all the change in the world will help you identify impermanence in action and give you a variety of things to focus on.

Sit outside or near a window, and leave the eyes open. Set the intention to rest in awareness of your present-time experience. Place the awareness on the body and the breath, taking in where you are and how you are sitting. Begin by noticing where you can feel motion in the body as you sit still. Rest with the breath and pay attention to the abdomen, chest, shoulders, and anywhere else you can sense the change

Open to your sense of hearing. Notice the presence of any noises, speci cally tuning in to their changing nature. You may hear cars coming and going, your breath owing in and out, birds chirping and stopping, or any other sounds as they rise and eventually fade away. When a sound comes into your awareness, focus on it for a few moments before opening up to other sounds again.

Finally, use your sense of sight and see the movement in the world. What can you see that is moving or changing? There may be obvious movement, like cars driving, trees blowing in the wind, or people on the move. You may also notice subtle signs of movement and change, like the browning leaves of autumn, clouds oating across the sky, or a pothole that has been growing.

35
Color Your World

The world is full of different colors, and you can practice mindfulness by paying attention to which ones you are seeing in the present moment. Seeing is a different experience from tuning in to the breath or body, but it offers the same opportunity to be deeply present. We rely heavily on our sense of sight, making it a powerful tool for the cultivation of mindfulness.

You can do this practice anywhere. You may be sitting at your desk, taking a ride on the bus, or walking down the street. Wherever you decide to do this practice, set aside 10 minutes to dedicate yourself to it.

Arrive in the present moment. Take a few mindful breaths, feel the body where it is, and allow your energy to settle.

Pick one color to focus on. You may try starting with red one day, and work your way through the traditional rainbow spectrum on each subsequent day.

Find one thing you can see that is the color you have picked. Look at it with beginner's mind, as if you have never seen this thing before. Note what it is and its size and shape. After a few moments, look for something else that is this color. Observe this object in the same way.

Continuing with this practice, notice when your mind wanders o . You can always return to the sensation of breathing, using the breath as the anchor for your awareness. You may nd it helpful to mentally note exactly what you are seeing. For example, a red stop sign doesn't get labeled "red stop sign"; it becomes "red, octagon, writing, metal."

When 10 minutes have passed, allow the eyes to close for a moment. Take a few deep breaths, let go of the practice, and return to your daily life

A DAY OF COLORING: You can modify this practice a bit to incorporate it throughout your day. Pick a color and use it as an awareness trigger (see Exercise 26, The Awareness Trigger). Keep this color in mind through-out your day, and just notice whenever you see it. This practice can remind you to stay present during your day or to return to mindfulness as you get caught up in your day-to-day activities

36
Dedicated Listening

This exercise requires a partner. Ask a friend or loved one to join you for 10 minutes of practice. They may be a complete beginner to mindfulness or have a practice of their own. It doesn't matter!
In this exercise, you both will be working with the practice of listening mindfully. Whomever you choose, they should be somebody you trust. The practice will require some vulnerability.
The partner who is listening should listen attentively, with a clear mind and no judgment. Try to be present with the experience of listening, and let go of the need to respond. While listening, you should retain awareness of your own experience as you take in the words the other is saying. Explore what it means to be present while listening.
When speaking, practice mindful speech. Be honest, allow yourself to be vulnerable, and observe the words you are saying.

Sit down at eye level with your partner. Choose one person to speak rst while the other listens. Set a timer for four minutes. The person who speaks rst can begin talking about goals and intentions they have—for their day, for their loved ones, for their future, and so on. When the timer goes o , switch roles. The other person can now talk about their goals and intentions, while the other person practices mindful listening.

When the timer completes, spend a few minutes conversing. How was the practice? What was it like to sit and just listen? Was it di cult to not respond?

37
Mindful Bathing

Showering and bathing are common times to check out. You let your mind wander, go completely into autopilot, or just shut down mentally. Instead, you can use this time to work on your mindfulness practice. Make your shower time a cleansing ritual for the body and the mind, using the prompts in this exercise. You can practice with any or all of your senses in the shower, but for this practice, you will focus primarily on the physical body.

Begin your practice before turning on the water. Stand for a moment and bring your awareness to the rising and falling of the breath in the chest. Feel the lungs expand and contract with each inhalation and exhalation.

As you turn on the water, feel your hands on the knob, watch the water begin to ow, and hear the noise of the shower. Notice if heat or steam lls the room. Once you step into the shower, acknowledge what you are feeling. You may notice the temperature change, the sensation of water on the skin, and any response of the body to the water.

Go through your usual routine, feeling the movement, texture, and points of contact in the body. Rest your attention on the hands and skin as you wash and rinse your body. Moving more slowly than you normally do will help the mind stay present.

Wrapping up the showering process, don't let your awareness go. Stay present as you shut the water o and get out. Feel the towel on your skin as you dry yourself. Moving on with your day, try to retain this awareness of the body.

9 7 9 8 7 2 2 9 4 0 3 3 9